AF431129

Copyright 2022 © Illustrated by URBANTOONS
Publishing All rights reserved By Urbantoons Inc. No part of this publication may be reproduced, distributed, or transmitted in any form or by any means, including photocopying, recording, or other electronic or mechanical methods, without the prior written permission(permission) of the publisher, except in the case of brief quotations bodied in critical reviews and certain other noncommercial uses permitted by copyright law. For permission requests, write to the publisher, addressed "Attention: Permissions Coordinator," at the email address below. URBANTOONS Publishing urbantoonkids@gmail.com www.urbantoons.com Publisher's Note: This is a work of fiction. Names, characters, places, and incidents are a product of the author's imagination. Locales and public names are sometimes used for atmospheric purposes. Any resemblance to actual people, living

or dead, businesses, companies, events, institutions, or locales is completely coincidental.

Urbantoons

KWANZAA

Kwanzaa, Kwanzaa
A holiday so grand
Celebrating our heritage
With seven principles in hand

First is

Umoja

Unity we strive for
Together we stand strong
As one family and more

Second is

Kujichagulia

Self-determination our goal
Taking control of our own destinies
With determination in our souls

Third is

Ujima

Collective work and responsibility
Helping each other along the way
For a brighter future, we all agree

TEAM WORK!
RULE #1
THERE IS NO "I" IN
TEAM!

Fourth is

Ujamaa

Cooperative economics we embrace
Supporting our own communities
And the businesses we face

gic
FREE Home Secu
System!

Fifth is

Nia

Purpose in all that we do
Fulfilling our dreams
And staying true to our roots

Sixth is

Kuumba

Creativity in all that we make
Beautifying our world
For the future's sake

Seventh is

Imani

Faith in our abilities
Believing in ourselves
And achieving our goals with ease

GOALS
1. DO BUSINESS IN AFRICA
2. SELL BOOKS ACROSS THE WORLD.
3. 3D ANIMATION
4. VR BOOKS

A time to reflect
On the principles that guide us
As we continue to connect
With family and friends
We celebrate this joyous season
Honoring our heritage
And embracing our reason.

The End

www.ingramcontent.com/pod-product-compliance
Lightning Source LLC
Chambersburg PA
CBHW042135110726
48006CB00003B/888